Louisiana
Facts and Symbols

by Emily McAuliffe

Consultant:
Robert Rome
Louisiana Council for Social Studies

Hilltop Books
an imprint of Franklin Watts
A Division of Grolier Publishing
New York   London   Hong Kong   Sydney
Danbury, Connecticut

Hilltop Books
http://publishing.grolier.com

Library of Congress Cataloging-in-Publication Data
McAuliffe, Emily.
   Louisiana facts and symbols/by Emily McAuliffe.
   p.cm.—(The states and their symbols)
   Includes bibliographical references and index.
   Summary: Presents information about the state of Louisiana and its nickname,
motto, and emblems.
   ISBN 0-7368-0081-6
   1. Emblems, State—Louisiana—Juvenile literature. [1. Emblems, State—Louisiana.
2. Louisiana.] I. Title. II. Series: McAuliffe, Emily. States and their symbols.
CR203.L68M33 1999
976.3—dc21
                                                                    98-16600
                                                                        CIP
                                                                        AC

Editorial Credits
Mark Drew, editor; James Franklin, cover designer and illustrator; Sheri Gosewisch
   photo researcher

Photo Credits
American Catahoula Association, 18
Borland Stock Photo/Charlie Borland, 10
Henry C. Aldrich, 16
Louisiana State Museum, 22 (top)
Lynn M. Stone, 12
One Mile Up Inc., 8, 10 (inset)
Photri Microstock/Dennis MacDonald, 6
Root Resources/Mary A. Root, cover
Steve C. Healy, 22 (middle)
Unicorn Stock Photos/Martha McBride, 14; Kimberly Burnham, 22 (bottom)
Visuals Unlimited/David G. Campbell, 20

Table of Contents

Arkansas

LOUISIANA

Texas

Mississippi River

Mississippi

Atchafalaya River

Atchafalaya Basin

Baton Rouge
⭐

Louisiana
State Museum

**New
Orleans**

Aquarium
of the Americas

Gulf of Mexico

○ City
⭐ Capital
〰 River
🏛 Places to
  Visit

Fast Facts about Louisiana

Capital: Baton Rouge is Louisiana's capital.

Largest City: Louisiana's largest city is New Orleans. About 500,000 people live in New Orleans.

Size: Louisiana covers 51,843 square miles (134,273 square kilometers).

Location: Louisiana is in the southern United States.

Population: 4,351,769 people live in Louisiana (U.S. Census Bureau, 1997 estimate).

Statehood: Louisiana became the 18th state on April 30, 1812.

Natural Resources: Louisiana has oil, natural gas, salt, and sulfur.

Manufactured Goods: Louisianians make chemicals, gasoline, and foods.

Crops: Louisiana farmers grow soybeans, cotton, and sugarcane. They also raise cattle, pigs, and sheep.

State Name and Nickname

French explorer René-Robert Cavalier, Sieur de La Salle gave Louisiana its name. La Salle traveled to the mouth of the Mississippi River in 1682. He named the land he found there La Louisianne. La Salle chose this name to honor France's king Louis the 14th.

Many people call Louisiana the Bayou State. Louisiana has many bayous. These slow-moving streams flow through many of Louisiana's swamps. A swamp is a wetland with spongy ground and thick plant growth.

Some people call Louisiana the Fisherman's Paradise. People catch many fish in Louisiana. Others call Louisiana the Pelican State. A pelican is a large waterbird. Brown pelicans are common on Louisiana's coast.

Louisiana has many bayous.

STATE OF LOUISIANA

UNION · JUSTICE

· CONFIDENCE ·

State Seal and Motto

Louisiana adopted its state seal in 1902. The state seal is a symbol. It reminds Louisianians of their state's government. The seal also makes government papers official.

Louisiana's state seal shows an adult pelican feeding three young pelicans. The adult pelican stands for Louisiana's state government. The young pelicans stand for Louisiana's citizens. The seal suggests that Louisiana's state government provides for its citizens. The seal also suggests that the government keeps Louisianians safe.

Louisiana's state motto is "Union, justice, and confidence." A motto is a word or saying that people believe in. Union means Louisiana is part of the United States. Justice means Louisiana's government is fair to its people. Confidence means Louisianians have faith in themselves and their state government.

Louisiana adopted its state seal in 1902.

State Capitol and Flag

Louisiana's capitol building is in Baton Rouge. Baton Rouge is the capital of Louisiana. Government officials work in the capitol. They meet there to make the state's laws.

Louisiana's capitol has a 450-foot (137-meter) tower. The tower has 34 floors. Government officials have offices in the tower.

Workers started building Louisiana's capitol in 1930. They finished in 1932. The capitol cost more than 4 million dollars.

The Louisiana government adopted the state flag in 1912. The flag is blue. The pelicans from the state seal appear in the flag's center. Louisiana's motto appears beneath the pelicans.

Louisiana's capitol building is in Baton Rouge.

State Bird

The brown pelican became Louisiana's state bird in 1966. Brown pelicans are three and one-half to four feet (1.1 to 1.2 meters) long. Their wings may measure up to seven feet (2.1 meters) across. Brown pelicans are mostly gray-brown. They have white heads and yellow foreheads.

Brown pelicans have large bills with deep pouches. They use their bills to catch fish. Brown pelicans fly low above the ocean when they hunt. They dive when they see fish. They scoop the fish with their bills. Brown pelicans store the fish they catch in their pouches.

Brown pelicans build nests near other pelicans. The nests usually rest on the ground or in low trees. Female pelicans lay two or three eggs in their nests each year.

Brown pelicans use their large bills to catch fish.

State Tree

The bald cypress became Louisiana's state tree in 1963. Most cypress trees have leaves all year. Bald cypress trees lose their leaves during winter. This is how the trees received their name.

Louisiana's bald cypress trees can grow to be 120 feet (37 meters) tall. They have red-brown bark and short leaves. Their leaves look like pine needles. Bald cypress trees produce cones. The cones hold bald cypress seeds.

Bald cypress trees grow well near Louisiana's bayous, swamps, and rivers. Some bald cypress trees grow in water. Bald cypress trees growing in water sometimes have bumps on their roots. These bumps are called knees.

Bald cypress knees stick out of the water. They provide air for the roots. Some bald cypress knees grow into strange shapes.

Bald cypress trees growing in water sometimes have bumps on their roots. These bumps are called knees.

State Flower

Louisiana's state flower is the magnolia blossom. The Louisiana government chose the magnolia blossom in 1900.

Magnolia blossoms are large, white flowers. They can grow to be 10 inches (25 centimeters) across. They have six to 12 petals. Petals are the colored outer parts of flowers.

In Louisiana, magnolia blossoms bloom during early summer. The blossoms are famous for their strong, sweet scent.

Magnolia blossoms grow on magnolia trees. There are many magnolia trees in the southeastern United States. They can grow to be 60 to 80 feet (18 to 24 meters) tall. Magnolia trees produce large, oval leaves. The leaves are shiny. They stay green all year long.

Magnolia blossoms are large, white flowers.

State Dog

The Catahoula (KAT-uh-HOO-luh) leopard dog is Louisiana's state dog. It became the state dog in 1979.

Catahoula leopard dogs are native to Louisiana. They are named after a parish in southeastern Louisiana. In Louisiana, a parish is a county.

Adult Catahoulas can grow to be 20 to 26 inches (51 to 66 centimeters) tall. They weigh 40 to 50 pounds (18 to 23 kilograms). Catahoulas have short, thick coats. Their coats can be many colors. Some catahoulas have spots on their coats.

Catahoulas have webbed feet. Skin connects their toes. Webbed feet make Catahoula leopard dogs strong swimmers.

Catahoula leopard dogs make good pets and guard dogs. Catahoulas also are excellent hunting and work dogs. They help farmers find stray pigs and cattle.

Catahoula leopard dogs are native to Louisiana.

More State Symbols

State Reptile: The alligator became Louisiana's state reptile in 1983. Many alligators live in Louisiana's swamps and bayous.

State Crustacean: The crawfish became the state crustacean in 1983. Crawfish look like small lobsters. People in Louisiana like to eat crawfish.

State Insect: The honeybee became Louisiana's state insect in 1977. Many people in Louisiana raise honeybees for honey. Louisianians collect thousands of pounds of honey each year.

State Wildflower: The Louisiana iris became Louisiana's state wildflower in 1990. Louisiana irises grow in wet areas. They have red-orange petals and long stems.

State Doughnut: The beignet (ben-YAY) became Louisiana's state doughnut in 1986. A beignet is a square, puffy doughnut sprinkled with powdered sugar. It does not have a hole in the middle.

The alligator is Louisiana's state reptile.

Places to Visit

Louisiana State Museum

The Louisiana State Museum is in New Orleans. The museum is in eight historic buildings. Visitors learn about Louisiana's history and the history of jazz. Jazz is a type of music that began in New Orleans.

Aquarium of the Americas

The Aquarium of the Americas is in New Orleans. It stands on the bank of the Mississippi River. The aquarium has more than 7,000 underwater animals. Visitors see fish, reptiles, and birds in their natural surroundings.

Atchafalaya Basin

The Atchafalaya (uh-cha-fuh-LYE-uh) Basin is a large swamp in southeastern Louisiana. It stretches along the Atchafalaya River. The Atchafalaya Basin is home to many kinds of wildlife. Visitors canoe and fish in the basin. They also take guided swamp tours.

Words to Know

bayou (BYE-oo)—a slow-moving stream that runs through a swamp; bayous usually flow to or from lakes and rivers.

beignet (ben-YAY)—a square, puffy doughnut sprinkled with powdered sugar

explorer (ek-SPLOR-ur)—a person who travels to discover what a place is like

parish (PAR-ish)—in Louisiana, a county

pelican (PEL-uh-kuhn)—a large waterbird

swamp (SWAHMP)—a wetland with spongy ground and thick plant growth

symbol (SIM-buhl)—an object that reminds people of something else; the U.S. flag is a symbol of the United States.

Read More

Bock, Judy and Rachel Kranz. *Scholastic Encyclopedia of the United States.* New York: Scholastic, 1997.

Capstone Press Geography Department. *Louisiana.* One Nation. Mankato, Minn.: Capstone Press, 1996.

Fradin, Dennis B. *Louisiana.* From Sea to Shining Sea. Chicago: Children's Press, 1995.

LaDoux, Rita C. *Louisiana.* Hello U.S.A. Minneapolis: Lerner Publications, 1993.

Useful Addresses

Department of Culture, Recreation, and Tourism
State Capitol Building
Baton Rouge, LA 70804

Louisiana Secretary of State
3851 Essen Lane
Baton Rouge, LA 70809

Internet Sites

The Audubon Institute
http://www.auduboninstitute.org
Louisiana Cultural & Historical Information
http://crt.state.la.us/crt/sbcover.htm
Louisiana Information for Students
http://www.state.la.us/state/student.htm

Index